GAMBLING ADDICTION

ACKNOWLEDGE

UNDERSTAND

PREVENTION

RESOLUTION

A Self-Discovery workbook

Rui M. Lima, MA, MSW, LICSW

2018

©

DEDICATION

**This workbook is dedicated to the people who struggle with addiction,
to the people who found the understanding, determination,
attitude and resolution to discover their inner strengths
and sublime self-control**

RUI M. LIMA, MA, MSW, LICSW

I wrote this gambling addiction workbook to explore ways to deal with daily challenges, increase self-understanding of life purposes, and fulfill the synchronization of sublime emotions.

We are the way we perceive and feel the universe. The way we use our emotions determines our capacity to organize our thoughts and live a troubled or peaceful life. We self-discover the dynamics of our motivations and inner selves by recognizing the roots of our thoughts, attitudes and behaviors, and by fostering the process of assertiveness, self-awareness, self-care, self-regulation, self-actualization, insight, hope, healing, and transformation.

You will challenge your belief system, overwhelming behaviors, and misunderstood feelings and thoughts, when completing this workbook. You will identify physical, emotional and cognitive cues that may trigger unwanted behaviors, such as uncontrollable, unmanageable gambling, and master the application of mindfulness and self-control. You will learn relapse prevention, stress and anger management, conflict resolution, decision making, grief and loss, problem solving, assertiveness, healthy communication skills, and mindfulness coping skills. You will be able to demonstrate knowledge of application of coping skills with others, with your psychotherapist or in group. You will comprehend the underlying forces of healthy and unhealthy relationships, and improve your interpersonal relationships.

I have learned that personal awareness and growth leads to an increase sense of identity, personal power, creativity, and greater purpose. The goal of this workbook is to have you acknowledge your strengths through your own self-discovery from your childhood to the present time, and reveal fundamental components that will assist you in recognizing the true meaning of your life without addiction. You will understand how environment and circumstances affect behaviors, and how powerful inner motivations make the person you became.

I hold a Masters of Arts degree in Rehabilitation Counseling from Assumption College, and a Master of Social Work degree from Bridgewater State University. I am a Licensed Independent Clinical Social Worker in the states of Massachusetts and Rhode Island.

My experience as a psychotherapist includes the use of mindfulness and eclectic psychotherapy to address fluctuations in mood, addictions, and feelings of dissatisfaction with self, with relationships, and with work.

Table of Contents

"Nothing goes away until has taught us what we need to know."

Buddha

INTRODUCTION TO GAMBLING ADDICTION WORKBOOK

Uncontrollable and unmanageable gambling may cause painful emotions and chaos in your life. You will gain self-control by understanding the roots of your gambling addiction and obsessions.

It is our reactions that show our self-control or lack of it. We must acquire self-control if we want to have a life free of addictions and obsessions. We must embrace mindfulness approaches, and increase awareness of cognitive and physical cues that may trigger addiction and obsession behaviors, such as gambling.

We become the thoughts that we act upon. Our behaviors may determine the level of consciousness of our physical and psychological desires, fears and pains. We must ask ourselves what has been causing emptiness, desires, pains and fears. What have we done to conquer our desires, fears and pains?

It is imperative that you are honest with yourself and others. It is vital that you stop lying to yourself by predicting probabilities, magically guessing by observing colors, numbers, shapes, environments, and other delusional influences.

You must convince yourself that you cannot predict the future or outcome of gambling occurrences.

- **How much control do you have over your gambling? Please circle one.**

0	1	2	3	4	5	6	7	8	9	10	+
None										Extremely	

Please explain your choice: _______________________________________

____

____

The motivation to change comes from inside of us. Everything we do is motivated by something internal or external. Motivation is for human beings what fuel is for vehicles. Our desire to change may be influenced by internal understanding and grow by external and environmental factors. We are our true motivators when we honestly seek our true selves.

- **How motivated are you to stop gambling? Please circle one.**

0	1	2	3	4	5	6	7	8	9	10	+
None										Extremely	

Please explain your choice: _______________________________________

____

YOU

People lose their health, their wealth, their family, relationships, their loved ones, their sense of self, their purpose in life, and even their lives due to addiction.

Please describe everything you know about yourself from birth until the current time and how addiction interferes with your happiness. Include your interactions with childhood friends, family dynamics, school encounters, romantic relationships, work environment, legal and illegal activities, events that led to trouble with the law, and behaviors that resulted in chaotic lifestyle. Additionally, include other experiences and events that shaped the person you are today. Please write about who, when, where, why, and how you first experience chaos in your life due to addiction. It is important to be honest in your comments, opinions, and observations. Your memory will assist in understanding the birth of your addiction.

____

____

____

____

____

____

____

____

____

____

____

____

____

____

____

____

____

____

____

____

SELF-DISCOVERY

We grow healthy emotionally when we have complete self-awareness and understanding of our inner selves' strengths and life purposes. Self-control is gained by application of mindfulness knowledge and experience of the self.

- **How much Self-control do you currently have? Please circle one.**

0	1	2	3	4	5	6	7	8	9	10	+

No
Self-control

Extremely Self-Control

Please explain your choice: _______________________________

____

____

- **How much did you loss because of your addiction? Please circle one.**

0	1	2	3	4	5	6	7	8	9	10	+

Lost
Nothing

Lost a lot

Please explain your choice: _______________________________

____

____

- **How much do you love and care about yourself? Please circle one.**

0	1	2	3	4	5	6	7	8	9	10	+

Do not
Love or Care

Extremely Love & Care

Please explain your choice: _______________________________

____

- **How much you care about your family? Please circle one.**

0	1	2	3	4	5	6	7	8	9	10	+

Don't
care

Extremely care

Please explain your choice: _______________________________

____

We must self-motivate, love and care about ourselves and others, and apply what is known as beneficial to our inner selves. We must learn, participate, understand and enrich the following:

- Self-understanding   (needs, purposes, goals, objectives)
- Self-care   (body, mind, emotionally, spirituality)
- Self-awareness   (past and present)
- Self-direction   (motivation, beneficial way)
- Self- commitment   (contract, promise)
- Self-change   (courage, determination, ownership)
- Self- responsibility   (fairness, justice, morality, integrity)
- Self-love   (unconditionally)
- Self-accountability   (fearlessness, honesty)
- Self-flexibility   (workable; dependable)
- Self-insight   (visionary, awake)
- Self-discovery   (finding, hope)
- Self-motivation   (genuine enthusiasm)
- Self-discipline   (control, happiness)
- Self-empowerment   (inner force, energy)
- Self-esteem   (capability, belief)
- Self-reliance   (confidence, thrust)
- Self-acceptance   (awareness of strength, happiness)
- Self-worth   (value, respect)
- Self-realization   (__________________________________)
- Self-healing   (__________________________________)
- Self-actualization   (__________________________________)
- Self-regulation   (__________________________________)
- Self-control   (__________________________________)

Sometimes the demands of repetition, failure, chaotic lifestyle, painful experiences, careless thoughts, abusive relationships, and impulsive behaviors, lead us to change and learn healthy coping skills. We must hold on to self-acceptance, self-responsibility, self-accountability, and self-discipline, in order to prevent, understand and find resolution for our problems.

- **How motivated are you to learn healthy coping skills to deal with your gambling addiction? Please circle one.**

0	1	2	3	4	5	6	7	8	9	10	+

Not motivated   Very motivated

Please explain your choice: ____

____

____

Be the positive energy that connects you to the universe

In order to remain free of self-destructive thoughts and behaviors, we must discover ourselves and acquire full knowledge about ourselves. We must seek our guiding manual and master our desires. We must understand the roots of our suffering and identify our strengths. We must comprehend, believe, and integrate into our sense of being human, the greater purpose of our lives, without addictive, obsessive and destructive behaviors.

Please check what it is important to you:

√		√		√		√		
Relationships	Strength	Culture	Honesty	Creativity	
Universe	Inner self	Reason	Fitness	Media	
Intimacy	Data	Introvert	Health	Travel	
Leisure	Nature	Money	Appearance	Drugs	
Independence	Education	Trustworthy	Control	Virtue	
Money	Young-self	Acceptance	Religion	Image	
Art	Input	Love	Joy	Sexuality	
Internet	Socialize	Impossible	Risks	Exercise	
Space	Mother	Sincere	Fun	Training	
Awareness	Yearns	Mystical	Play	Motivation	
Growth	Life	Able	Humor	Flexibility	
Rigidity	Openness	Real	Family	Transportation	
Energy	Values	Violence	Friends	Shelter	
Acceptance	Gambling	Experience	Obligations	Food	
Talents	Theories	Lucrative	Work	Hobbies	
Morals	Occult	Office	Sex	Time	
Assurance	Oxygen	Uniqueness	Race	Faith	
Needs	Trust	Sun glasses	Gender	Self-control	
Time	Drugs	Today	Things	Alcohol	
People	Drinking	Ambition	Places	Clothing	
Addiction	Nothing	Goals	Death	Tomorrow	

√		Please add	√
Responsibility	Other:__________________	
Accountability	Other:__________________	
Self-determination	Other:__________________	
Self-actualization	Other:__________________	
School	Other:__________________	
Self-regulation	Other:__________________	
Self-esteem	Other:__________________	
Articulateness	Other:__________________	
Self-control	__________________	

WHO ARE YOU?

Name: ____ Age: ______________

Gender: ______________ Birth Date: ________________SSN: ______________

Height: ____________ Weight: _________

Who gave you your name? ____

What is the meaning of your name? ____

- **How much do you know yourself? Please circle one.**

0	1	2	3	4	5	6	7	8	9	10	+
Do not										**Extremely**	

Please explain your choice: ____

____

Ethnic Group:

1. African American/ Black___   2.Azorean___   4. French___ 5.German___

6. Hispanic / Latino___   7.Italian___   8.Irish ___ 9. Native American___

10. Portuguese___   11. Other: ____

Race:

1. American Indian/ Native American___ 2. African American/ Black___ 3.Asian____

3. White Caucasian____ 4.Bi-Racial: ____

5. Other: ____

Sexual Orientation:

( ) Heterosexual ( ) Bisexual ( ) Homosexual ( ) Transgender   ( ) pan-sexual

( ) Other: ____

A) What are your Strengths?

____
____
____
____
____
____
____

B) What are your Abilities and Skills? (e.g. vocational)

____
____
____
____
____
____
____

C) What are your Needs?

____
____
____
____
____
____
____
____

D) What are your Goals? (What would you like to accomplish in one month; three
months, six months, one year, two years, and five years).

____

____

____

____

____

____

____

____

____

E) What are the favorite things you like to do in your free time and with whom? (e.g.
hobbies, sports, family involvement, etc.).

____

____

____

____

F) Please write everything you would like to change in your life.

____

____

____

____

____

____

____

G) Please describe all your achievements?

____

____

____

____

____

____

H) Please write everything you have lost due to your gambling.

____

____

____

____

____

____

____

____

____

____

____

____

____

____

<u>**ENVIRONMENT**</u>

1. Where do you live?

City: ________________________ State:___________ Zip: ________

<u>**Household / Living Arrangements:**</u>

1. House/Apartment__ 2. Group Home__ 3. Room/Boarding house__ 4. Shelter__

5. Other: ____

1. How many times have you moved in the last year? ______________

2. Do you feel you live in a safe place? YES/NO (Please circle one)

Please explain:

____

____

____

____

3. Who lives with you?

____

____

____

____

4. In the past year, has your partner, family member, or stranger pushed you, punched you, kicked you, hit you, or threatened to hurt you? YES/NO (Please circle one)

If yes, who: ________________________ When: ____________________________

Why: ____

____

____

____

<u>**RELATIONSHIP STATUS:**</u>

( ) Never married ( ) Single ( ) Married ( ) Separated ( ) Divorced ( ) Widowed

1. How many children do you have? _______With how many partners: ________

2. What are their ages and gender? ____

3. Where do your children live now?

____

____

4. Who takes care of your children?

____

____

____

5. Did you neglect your children due to legal problems? YES/NO. Please explain.

____

____

____

6. Are you currently in a romantic relationship? YES/NO (Please circle one)

Please explain: ____

____

7. Does your partner had an addiction? YES/NO (Please circle one)

Please explain: ____

____

8. Does your partner have or had anger issues? YES/NO (Please circle one)

Please explain: ____

____

9. How long have you been with your partner?

____

10. What do you do for fun with your partner?

____

____

____

11. How did you meet your current partner?

____

____

____

12. What have you learnt with your partner?

____

____

____

13. How many friends do you have? ____________________

14. How many acquaintances you have? _________________

15. How many friends do you have who have an addiction? __________

16. How many of your friends gamble? ___________________________

17. How many friends do you have who are currently using illegal drugs? ____________

18. How many friends do you have who had overdosed in drugs? __________________

19. How many of your friends do have a job? ________________________________

20. How many of your friends use cannabis? ________________________________

21. How many of your friends drink alcohol? ________________________________

22. How many of your friends attend self-help groups? ___________________

23. How many of your friends have been in prison? ____________________________

24. How many of your friends are violent? ________________________________

25. How many of your friends have unhealthy relationship? _______________________

26. How many of your friends have anger issues? _______________________________

27. How many of your friends have been victims of abuse? ________________________

28. How many of your friends are abusers? ________________________________

29. How do you describe your friends?

____

____

____

____

30. What did you learn with your friends and family members? Please elaborate the good, the bad, and the ugly that you have experienced and learned from your friends and family members.

____

____

____

____

____

____

____

____

____

____

____

____

____

____

____

21. Were you popular in school or in your neighborhood? YES/NO (Please circle one) Please elaborate.

____

____

____

____

____

WHEN YOU WERE A CHILD

1. Did either parent have an addiction problem? YES/NO (Please circle one)
If yes, who? How long was the problem? What do you remember about the problem?
How has this problem affected your life as a child and now as an adult?

____

____

____

____

____

____

____

2. Were you exposed to domestic violence growing up? YES/NO (Please circle one)
If yes, what do you remember about it? How do you think violence affected your life
as a child and now as an adult?

____

____

____

____

____

____

3. Were you raised in part or all of the time by foster parents or relatives? (Other
than your parents) YES/NO. Please explain.

____

____

____

4. How often did your parents/guardians ground you or put you in time out?   Please
elaborate
( ) Frequently   ( ) Often   ( ) Occasionally   ( ) Rarely   ( ) Never

____

____

5. Do you feel you were physically abused   YES/NO

____

____

____

6. Do you feel you were neglected?   YES/NO

____

____

____

7. Do you feel you were hurt in a sexual way?   YES/NO

____

____

____

8. Did your parents ever hurt you when they were out of control?   YES/NO

____

____

____

EARLY FAMILY

1. Did you live in a two-parent family? YES/NO. If yes until when?

____

____

____

If no, why not? ____

____

____

____

____

2. Do you have siblings? YES/NO. If yes, how many? _______________________

    Did they live in the same family? YES/NO. If no, why not?

    ____

    ____

    ____

3. Do you get along with your siblings? YES/NO. Please elaborate.

    ____

    ____

4. Did your family have ongoing family difficulties? YES/NO. If yes, please
    explain.

    ____

    ____

    ____

5. Did you like school? YES/NO. If yes, please explain.

    ____

    ____

6. Did you have difficulties at school? YES/NO. If yes, please explain.

    ____

    ____

    ____

7. Did you have behavior problems at school? YES/NO. If yes, please explain.

    ____

    ____

    ____

8. Were you bullied at school? YES/NO. If yes, please explain.

    ____

    ____

    ____

9. How many fights did you have with your peers at school? _______________
    Please explain

    ____

    ____

    ____

CURRENT FAMILY PROFILE

1. Who lives with you?

____

____

____

2. How do you describe your relationship with your parents?

____

____

____

3. How do you describe your relationship with your partner?

____

____

____

____

4. How do you describe your relationship with your sibling(s)?

____

____

____

____

5. How do you describe your relationship with your children?

____

____

____

____

6. With whom do you talk about your problems?

____

____

7. Do you feel that you have a healthy support system? YES/NO. If yes, please explain

____

____

____

EDUCATION

1. How many years of school have you completed? ____________

   ( ) High school Diploma ( ) Some College ( ) College degree ( ) Other

2. What is the name of the last school you attended? ____________________

3. Would you like to return to school? YES/NO. Please explain.

   ____

   ____

4. What did you like about school? Please explain.

   ____

   ____

   ____

5. What did you dislike about school? Please explain.

   ____

   ____

   ____

6. Did you complete any certification programs? YES/NO. Please explain.

   ____

   ____

   ____

EMPLOYMENT

1. Are you employed? YES/NO. If YES, how long have you been employed?

   ____

2. What type of employment is it?

   ____

   ____

3. Where do you get your financial support?

   ____

4. Were you in the military? YES/NO. If YES, please explain.

   ____

LEISURE TIME ACTIVITY

1. What are the favorite things you do during your free time? With whom?

____

____

____

____

____

____

2. What activities are you involved within the community?

____

____

____

3. What would you like to do to have fun?

____

____

____

____

____

____

SPIRITUAL LIFE/CHURCH MEMBERSHIP

1. How strong are your family's religious beliefs or practices?
    ( ) Very Strong   ( ) Moderate strong ( ) Not strong   ( ) No religious

    What religion/Church/temple do you attend?

____

____

____

2. Is spirituality important in your life? YES/NO. Please explain.

____

____

____

FAMILY HISTORY

1. Has any member of your family been treated for PSYCHIATRIC problems?
YES/NO. If yes, who?

____

____

____

2. Has any member of your family been treated for MEDICAL problems? YES/NO.
If yes, who?

____

____

____

3. Has any member of your family been treated for SUBSTANCE ABUSE
problems? YES/NO. If yes, who?

____

____

4. Has any member of your family been involved with the legal system? YES/NO. If
yes, who?

____

____

____

5. Has any member of your family been involved with domestic violence or ANGER
MANAGEMENT programs? YES/NO. If yes, who?

____

____

____

FAMILY ACTIVITIES

1. What does your family do together for fun?

____

____

____

ANGER, ALCOHOL, DRUGS, GAMBLING AND JAIL

1. How many times have you been in trouble due to your anger? ______________
2. How many times did you use alcohol or drugs because of your anger? ______
3. Do you have a drug of choice? ____
4. How many times did you gamble intoxicated? ____________________________
5. How much did you spend a week in gambling? ____________________________
6. How many detoxes have you attended? __________________________________
7. How many times have you overdosed? __________________________________
8. How many times have you had a relapse? ________________________________
9. How long ago was your longest sobriety time? ________ and when? ______
10. How many times have you tried to cut down on gambling? ________________
11. How many times have you attended self-help groups? ___________________
12. How many times have you been on probation? __________________________
13. How many times have you been on parole? _____________________________
14. How many times have you been arrested? ______________________________
15. How many times have you been arrested? ______________________________
16. How many gambling programs have you attended? ______________________
17. How many half-way houses programs have you attended? ________________
16. Have you attended any of these programs?
    ( ) Gambling program
    ( ) Anger management
    ( ) Domestic violence
    ( ) Parenting
    ( ) Substance Abuse Program: ________________________________
    ( ) Mental Health Program: __________________________________
    ( ) Other: ____

Please explain when and where you completed programs:

____

____

____

17. How tired are you of doing the same things, falling for the same or similar
    problems, and expecting different results?

Please circle one.

0	1	2	3	4	5	6	7	8	9	10
Not Tired										Very Tired

Please explain: ____

____

HELP AND SUPPORT

1. Who can you count on to be dependable when you need help? (Write their initials and their relationship to you).
   a) ________________________ b) ________________________ c) ______________
   d) ________________________ e) ________________________ f) ______________

   ( ) If no one, explain.

   ____

   ____

2. How satisfied are you with their support?
   ( ) Very satisfied   ( ) Satisfied   ( ) Very dissatisfied   ( ) Dissatisfied
   ( ) No support

3. Who do you feel loves you deeply? (Please write their initials and their relationship to you).

   a) ____________________ b) ____________________ c) __________

   ( ) If no one, explain. ____

4. Are you currently involved or receiving services from the following?

   ( ) Department of Children and Family: __________________
   ( ) Probation: ____
   ( ) Parole: ____
   ( ) Department of Mental Health: ______________________
   ( ) Rehabilitation Services: ___________________________
   ( ) Court: ____
   ( ) Community Resources: ______________________________
   ( ) Other: ____
   ( ) Other: ____

5. Do you have an AA/NA sponsor? ________________________________
6. Do you have a pet? ____
7. Do you trust anybody? ____
8. Do you pray? ____
9. Do you talk to family members? _______________________________
10. Do you enjoy friendships? ____________________________________
11. Do you feel safe when in the company of close friends? Please explain.

____

____

____

MENTAL HEALTH AND SUBSTANCE ABUSE DISORDERS

1. Have you been diagnosed with a mental health disorder or/ and with a substance abuse disorder? YES/NO. Please explain.

____

____

____

____

2. Do you take medication due to a mental health disorder? YES/NO. Please explain.

____

____

____

____

3. Did you use to take medication due to a mental health disorder? YES/NO. Please explain.

____

____

____

____

4. Do you take medication due to a substance abuse disorder? YES/NO. Please explain.

____

____

____

____

5. Does medication help you with your mental health disorder? YES/NO. Please explain.

____

____

____

____

6. Do you agree about taking medication for a mental health disorder? YES/NO. Please explain.

____

____

____

7. Do you agree to take medication for a substance abuse disorder? YES/NO. Please explain.

____

____

____

____

8. How long have you been involved with psychiatric services? Please explain

____

____

____

____

9. In your opinion, what are the pros and cons of taking medications?

____

____

____

____

10. Do you have family members who take medication due to mental illness and/or substance abuse issues? YES/NO. Please explain.

____

____

____

____

11. Have you been diagnosed with any of the following? √ if yes, when?

    a) ( )Anxiety :____

    b) ( )Depression: ____

    c) ( )Mood disorder:____

    d) ( )PTSD: ____

    e) ( ) Borderline: ____

    f) ( )Anti-social:____

    g) ( )Avoidance: ____

    h) ( ) Schizophrenia: ____

    i) ( ) Other: ____

____

What are the most important aspects about yourself that you were able to identify by answering previous questions?

WORDS ABOUT FEELINGS

When we feel, we liberate life to its most beautiful human form. Feelings connect us to each other and to the universe. We are able to feel when we allow ourselves to receive the full magic and energy from life. Feelings are not good or bad, they are the amplitude of our needs. We can deeply engage in the process of self-discovery when we clarify our awareness and understanding about why we feel a certain way.

How do you feel today? √

Feeling	√	Feeling	√	Feeling	√	Feeling	√	Feeling	√	√
Awe		Aggravated		Caring		Blessed		Relieved		
Delighted		Disgruntled		Stimulated		Courageous		Inspired		
Playful		Adventurous		Yearning		Disturbed		Tender		
Calm		Contempt		Empathy		Grateful		Angry		
Centered		Cynical		Fascinated		Guilt		Miserable		
Thrusting		Valiant		Useless		Helpless		Overwhelmed		
Excited		Furious		Discouraged		Hesitant		Perplexed		
Accepting		Afraid		Appreciative		Humbled		Dread		
Enthusiastic		Frustrated		Disappointed		Impotent		Puzzled		
Engaged		Irritated		Anxious		Incapable		Detached		
Eager		Disturbed		Anguish		Joy		Helpful		
Relaxed		Daring		Indifferent		Nervous		Passive		
Renewed		Determined		Isolated		Panic		Aggressive		
Free		Grouchy		Grief		Perplexed		Troubled		
Ecstatic		Edgy		Depressed		Powerless		Curious		
Fulfilled		Hostile		Heartbroken		Questioning		Withdrawn		
Happy		Impatient		Hopeless		Rejecting		Uncomfortable		
Invigorated		Irate		Lonely		Reluctant		Embarrassed		
Rejuvenated		Confident		Distant		Remorseful		Intense		
Content		Disdain		Intrigued		Sad		Jealous		
Vibrant		Warm		Lucky		Safe		Detached		
Satisfied		Proud		Resistant		Scared		Insecure		
Radiant		Brave		Aloof		Self-loving		Open		
Amazed		Agitated		Affectionate		Sensitive		Peaceful		
Lively		Moody		Longing		Shocked		Zestful		
Mindful		Outraged		Melancholy		Skeptical		Mischievous		
Refreshed		Capable		Bored		Sorry		Alert		
Motivated		Resentful		Sorrow		Suspicious		Goofy		
Serene		Strong		Uneasy		Terrified		Distant		
Bliss		Bitter		Compassion		Thankful		Tranquil		
Patient		Upset		Unhappy		Ungrounded		Amorous		
Peaceful		Vindictive		Weary		Unsure		Friendly		
Thrilled		Worthy		Ashamed		Worried		Distracted		
Concerned		Annoyed		Surprised		Proud		Loved		

GAMBLING, FEELINGS AND THOUGHTS

1. What were the feelings and thoughts that you had **BEFORE** you last gambled? Please explain.

____

____

____

2. What were the feelings and thoughts that you had **AFTER** you last gambled? Please explain.

____

____

____

3. What were the feelings and thoughts that you were unable to control and understand **BEFORE** you last gambled? Please explain.

____

____

____

4. What were the feelings and thoughts that you were unable to control and understand **AFTER** you last gambled? Please explain.

____

____

____

____

5. What were the feelings and thoughts that made you accept that you have a gambling addiction? Please explain.

____

____

____

____

GAMBLING, BEHAVIORS AND ATTITUDES

1. What **ARE** the behaviors and attitudes that **CURRENTLY** hurt you and your family? Please explain.

____

____

____

____

2. What **ARE** the behaviors and attitudes that **CURRENTLY** hurt you emotionally? Please explain.

____

____

____

____

3. What **ARE** the behaviors and attitudes that **CURRENTLY** hurt your relationships? Please explain.

____

____

____

____

4. What **ARE** the behaviors and attitudes that **CURRENTLY** affect your work performance? Please explain.

____

____

____

____

5. What **ARE** the behaviors and attitudes that you are **CURRENTLY** unable to control? Please explain.

____

____

____

____

____

I AM

Who are you? Please complete the following:

I am ____.

I am ____.

I am ____.

I am ____.

I am ____.

I am ____.

I am ____.

I am ____.

I am ____.

I am ____.

I am ____.

I am ____.

I am ____.

I am ____.

I am ____.

I am ____.

I am ____.

I am ____.

I am ____.

I am ____.

I am ____.

I am ____.

I am ____.

I am ____.

I am ____.

I am ____.

I am ____.

I am ____.

I am ____.

I am ____.

WHEN I GAMBLE I...

Think about your emotions, attitudes and behaviors when you gamble, and complete the following:

When I gamble I ____.

When I gamble I ____.

When I gamble I ____.

When I gamble I ____.

When I gamble I ____.

When I gamble I ____.

When I gamble I ____.

When I gamble I ____.

When I gamble I ____.

When I gamble I ____.

When I gamble I ____.

When I gamble I ____.

When I gamble I ____.

When I gamble I ____.

When I gamble I ____.

When I gamble I ____.

When I gamble I ____.

When I gamble I ____.

When I gamble I ____.

When I gamble I ____.

When I gamble I ____.

When I gamble I ____.

When I gamble I ____.

When I gamble I ____.

When I gamble I ____.

When I gamble I ____.

When I gamble I ____.

ASSERTIVENESS

Assertive people are able to communicate their thoughts, needs, and feelings without offending others. They respect others rights and their own rights, and do not deny the right of others. Passive people tend to the needs of others before their own needs. Aggressive people definitely believe in their own rights but do not believe others have rights too.

1. **What style do you use when interacting with people?**
   The assertive style______
   The passive style________
   The aggressive style______

   Please explain your choice: ____

   ____

   ____

   ____

2. Are you happy with the decisions you make? YES/NO Please explain.

   ____

   ____

   ____

3. Do you think your needs are overlooked? YES/NO Please explain.

   ____

   ____

   ____

4. Do you think you deserve more respect? YES/NO Please explain.

   ____

   ____

   ____

5. Do you think you cooperate with others in a fair and consistent way? YES/NO
   Please explain.

   ____

   ____

   ____

6. My communication skills are______________________________________.

| 0 | 1 | 2 | 3 | 4 | 5 | 6 | 7 | 8 | 9 | 10 | + |

Poor   Excellent

Please explain.

____

____

____

7. Do you think you have the need to compete or prove yourself to others? YES/NO
   Please explain.

____

____

____

8. Do you have difficulty keeping affectionate / romantic relationships? YES/NO
   Please explain.

____

____

____

9. Do you assess situations and decide what action or behavior is most appropriate?
   YES/NO Please explain.

____

____

____

Please reflect about your answers and read the characteristics of each style.

ASSERTIVENESS	PASSIVE	AGGRESSIVE
Communicates well	Puts the needs of others first	Inappropriate behaviors
Appropriate behavior	Difficulty making decisions	Offensive and disrespectful
Respects others rights	Their needs are overlooked	Difficulty with relationships
Has self-control	Has low self-esteem	Poor communication skills
Direct and honest	May suffer from depression	Need to compete and prove
Polite and firm	May feel inferior to others	May have rude manners
Cooperative	Low self-respect	Hurtful and insulting

We must be assertive in order to increase control of our lives. We must be clear about what we want. We must be fair, consistent, honest, confident, flexible and able to compromise.

Apply these simple rules:

- Do not apologize or explain if you don't have to
- Use eye contact and calm voice
- Wait for your turn to speak
- Be clear, honest, and direct
- Recognize others rights and compromise if necessary or possible
- Don't except to convince
- Accept that life is not fair
- Be flexible and accept consequences
- Do not make excuses
- Pause and decide before replying
- Be aware of your body posture
- Be mindfulness of your surroundings
- Use I statements when necessary
- Do not be afraid to say No
- Be humble and firm
- Apply positive attitude
- Be knowledgeable about the subject of conversation
- Think before you open your mouth
- Select timing for conversations and environment
- Pay attention to details
- Value relationships and understand others stressors
- Validate others perceptions, valuable observations, and comments
- Agree and disagree without yelling or with an aggressive posture
- Ask for clarification when necessary
- Listen and focus what is actually being said
- Remain focus on the subject of discussion
- Acknowledge when you are wrong and apologize
- Select the level of your assertiveness with situation and person
- Positively practice what you had learned
- Always show respect and self-control
- Be polite and cooperate
- Understand others perceptions and attributes
- ____
- ____
- ____
- ____

I WANT TO HAVE...

Think about what you **WANT TO HAVE**. Please complete the following:

I want to have____.

I want to have____.

I want to have____.

I want to have____.

I want to have____.

I want to have____.

I want to have____.

I want to have____.

I want to have____.

I want to have____.

I want to have____.

I want to have____.

I want to have____.

I want to have____.

I want to have____.

I want to have____.

I want to have____.

I want to have____.

I want to have____.

I want to have____.

I want to have____.

I want to have____.

I want to have____.

I want to have____.

I want to have____.

I want to have____.

I NEED TO STOP GAMBLING IN ORDER TO HAVE....

Please complete the following:

I need to stop gambling in order to have_______________________________________.

I need to stop gambling in order to have_______________________________________.

I need to stop gambling in order to have_______________________________________.

I need to stop gambling in order to have_______________________________________.

I need to stop gambling in order to have_______________________________________.

I need to stop gambling in order to have_______________________________________.

I need to stop gambling in order to have_______________________________________.

I need to stop gambling in order to have_______________________________________.

I need to stop gambling in order to have_______________________________________.

I need to stop gambling in order to have_______________________________________.

I need to stop gambling in order to have_______________________________________.

I need to stop gambling in order to have_______________________________________.

I need to stop gambling in order to have_______________________________________.

I need to stop gambling in order to have_______________________________________.

I need to stop gambling in order to have_______________________________________.

I need to stop gambling in order to have_______________________________________.

I need to stop gambling in order to have_______________________________________.

I need to stop gambling in order to have_______________________________________.

I need to stop gambling in order to have_______________________________________.

I need to stop gambling in order to have_______________________________________.

I NEED...

Think about what you really **NEED** in your life.

Please complete the following:

I need ____.

I need ____.

I need ____.

I need ____.

I need ____.

I need ____.

I need ____.

I need ____.

I need ____.

I need ____.

I need ____.

I need ____.

I need ____.

I need ____.

I need ____.

I need ____.

I need ____.

I need ____.

I need ____.

I need ____.

I need ____.

I need ____.

I need ____.

I need ____.

I need ____.

I need ____.

I CARE ABOUT...

Think about what and who you deeply **CARE ABOUT.**

Please complete the following:

I care about____.

I care about____.

I care about____.

I care about____.

I care about____.

I care about____.

I care about____.

I care about____.

I care about____.

I care about____.

I care about____.

I care about____.

I care about____.

I care about____.

I care about____.

I care about____.

I care about____.

I care about____.

I care about____.

I care about____.

I care about____.

I care about____.

I care about____.

I care about____.

I care about____.

I DON'T CARE ABOUT...

Think about what you do not **CARE ABOUT.**

Please complete the following:

I don't care about____.

I don't care about____.

I don't care about____.

I don't care about____.

I don't care about____.

I don't care about____.

I don't care about____.

I don't care about____.

I don't care about____.

I don't care about____.

I don't care about____.

I don't care about____.

I don't care about____.

I don't care about____.

I don't care about____.

I don't care about____.

I don't care about____.

I don't care about____.

I don't care about____.

I don't care about____.

I don't care about____.

I don't care about____.

I don't care about____.

I don't care about____.

I don't care about____.

I don't care about____.

I WANT TO BE ...

Think about what you **WANT TO BE**.

Please complete the following:

I want to be ____.

I want to be ____.

I want to be ____.

I want to be ____.

I want to be ____.

I want to be ____.

I want to be ____.

I want to be ____.

I want to be ____.

I want to be ____.

I want to be ____.

I want to be ____.

I want to be ____.

I want to be ____.

I want to be ____.

I want to be ____.

I want to be ____.

I want to be ____.

I want to be ____.

I want to be ____.

I want to be ____.

I want to be ____.

I want to be ____.

I want to be ____.

I want to be ____.

I want to be ____.

GAMBLING, ANGER AND CONTROL

We had felt angry at least once about something or someone. How do we cope with anger? How do we manage frustration, provocation, irritation, disappointment, stress, conflict, and resentment? How do we identify physical, emotional and cognitive cues that may trigger these feelings?

There is no doubt that uncontrollable anger can lead to legal problems and damage relationships. We must recognize what causes or triggers anger, and deal with emotional and physical pain without gambling, drugs or alcohol. We must identify what is hurting inside of us in a therapeutic environment, and learn to forgive and heal. We must enhance consciousness of angry feelings by nourishing acceptance and recognizing the advantages of understanding, and forgiving past hurtful situations. We must forgive ourselves and others, and with determination move forward. We must improve our inner and interpersonal relationships, and maintain a positive attitude. We must increase comprehension of our body, mind, and emotion patterns, and apply mindfulness and self-control.

1. When you are angry do you gamble, use drugs or alcohol? YES/NO. Please explain.

____

____

____

2. Do you feel angry after gambling? YES/NO. Please explain.

____

____

____

3. How do you manage your anger?

____

____

____

4. How do you know when you are angry? What happens to you physically, mentally, emotionally?

Pysically:____

Mentally:____

Emotionally:____

Please indicate √ your symptoms of anger.

Physical Signs	**Mental Signs**	**Emotional Signs**	**Behavior**
Rapid heart beat	Rage	Racing thoughts	Running
Stomach ache	Aggressive thoughts	Overwhelmed	Violent
Sweating palms	Irritation	Anxious	Pacing
Tense Muscles	Confusion	Sad	Yelling
Tight Chest	Shutdown	Depressed	Spiting
Hot neck/ face	Disorganized thoughts	Nervous	Swearing
Clenching jaws	Guilt	Harmful thoughts	Throwing
Clenching teeth	Shame	Other:____________	Laughing
Dizziness	Lack of concentration	Other:____________	Passive
Tingling	Fantasies	Other:____________	Aggressive
Tight chest	Mood change		Assertive
Shaking	Other:________________		Indifferent
Headache	Other:________________		Gamble
Fatigue			Other;:____
Other:________________			Other:____

- **How difficult is for you to maintain self-control after having the above symptoms?**

0　1　2　3　4　5　6　7　8　9　**10**

Not Difficult　　　　　　　　　　　　　　　　　　**Very Difficult**

Please explain how the symptoms you identified impact your life.

____

____

____

____

____

____

5. List the **FIRST** signs you have noticed when you start getting angry.

Pysically:____

____

Mentally:____

____

Emotionally:____

____

6. What makes you angry? (e.g. not winning)

____

____

____

____

7. How do you react when you are angry? Please describe at least three past situations and how you reacted.

____

____

____

____

8.   Did you have legal issues because of your anger? YES/NO. Please describe past and present events.

____

____

____

____

9. What negative behaviors would you like to avoid when you are angry?

____

____

____

____

____

____

10. What is your plan to control your anger?

____

____

____

____

11. Identify eighteen positive reactions that you may practice to control your anger.
    (e.g. walk away, exercise)

1.____

2.____

3.____

4.____

5.____

6.____

7.____

8.____

9.____

10.____

11.____

12.____

13.____

14.____

15.____

16.____

17.____

18.____

12. **Please write below the people, things, places, and other stuff, damaged, lost or destroy due to your gambling.**

	People	Things	Places	Other
1.				
2.				
3.				
4.				
5.				
6.				
7.				
8.				
9.				
10.				
11.				
12.				

Please reflect, elaborate, and discuss what you wrote above.

____

____

____

____

____

____

____

____

____

____

____

GAMBLING AND CHANGE

1. Please write five characteristics that you would like to change about yourself in the next three months?

1.____

____

2.____

____

3.____

____

4.____

____

5.____

____

2. What motivates you to learn how to stop gambling? Please explain.

____

____

____

____

____

3. How will your life be if you stop gambling?

____

____

____

____

____

____

GAMBLING AND IMPULSE REACTIONS

Impulsive reactions, behaviors and attitudes, certainly can damage, offend, disrespect, provoke and result in predicaments with ourselves and others..

1. How impulsive were you as a child? Please circle one.

0	1	2	3	4	5	6	7	8	9	10 +

Not
Impulsive   Extremely Impulsive

Please explain your choice?

____

____

____

2. How impulsive are you NOW? Please circle one.

0	1	2	3	4	5	6	7	8	9	10

Not
Impulsive   Extremely Impulsive

Please explain your choice?

____

____

____

3. How much trouble have you had because of impulse attitudes and behaviors? Please circle one.

0	1	2	3	4	5	6	7	8	9	10 +

None   A lot

Please explain your choice?

____

____

____

GAMBLING, PEOPLE, PLACES, THINGS, EVENTS, THOUGHTS AND DESIRES

1. Please identify what may drive you to gamble(check any of the following that may apply): √

☐ Stress	☐ Inferiority feelings	☐ Low self-esteem
☐ Tension with others	☐ Grief	☐ Inability to make friends
☐ Pain	☐ Panic	☐ People
☐ Anxiety	☐ Fears and phobias	☐ Unhealthy relationships
☐ Depression	☐ Obsessions	☐ Inability to have a good time/fun
☐ Boredom	☐ Loneliness	☐ Places
☐ Physical pain	☐ Racing thoughts	☐ Inability to make decisions
☐ Lack of employment	☐ Traumatic experiences	☐ Disrespect
☐ Constant sleepiness	☐ Conflicts	☐ Legal problems
☐ Inability to relax	☐ Probation	☐ Financial problems
☐ Insomnia	☐ Parole	☐ Drugs
☐ Recurrent dreams	☐ Homeless	☐ Job problems
☐ Lack of money	☐ Sexual orientation	☐ Inability to keep a job
☐ Hallucinations	☐ Sexual problems	☐ Family problems
☐ Mood swings	☐ Medical problems	☐ Lack of self-care
☐ Peer pressure	☐ Unemployment	☐ Family
☐ Alcohol	☐ No satisfaction	☐ Other:_______________
☐ I want to be rich	☐ Addiction	☐ Other:_______________
☐ Legal problems	☐ Gamble since a child	☐ Other:
☐ Family used to gamble	☐ Challenge	☐ Other:

Other (Specify):

____

____

____

____

2. Please explain your choices.

____

____

____

____

____

____

GAMBLING, STRESS AND PLANNING ACTIVITIES

1. Please choose √ the activities that you think will be most helpful to assist you in reducing your daily stress.

☐ Meditating	☐ Praying	☐ Laughing
☐ Journaling	☐ Attending church	☐ Partying
☐ Finding hobbies	☐ Attending bible study	☐ Playing sports
☐ Attending self-help meetings	☐ Listening to music	☐ Spending time with family
☐ Attending AA meetings	☐ Reading a book, magazine	☐ Playing video games
☐ Attending NA meetings	☐ Watching TV	☐ Helping others
☐ Attending GA meetings	☐ Going to the park	☐ Eating your favorite food
☐ Going to the gym	☐ Going to the movies	☐ Treating yourself with new stuff
☐ Exercising with a friend	☐ Gardening	☐ Increasing romance
☐ Exercising alone	☐ Cleaning	☐ Dating
☐ Walking	☐ Washing	☐ Taking my partner out to dinner
☐ Talking to a friend	☐ Doing house chores	☐ Practicing mindfulness
☐ Talking to a family member	☐ Going for a ride	☐ Practicing Yoga
☐ Talking to your sponsor	☐ Shopping	☐ Other:_____________
☐ Talking to your counselor	☐ Attending school	☐ Other:

2. Please explain in detail how the activities you chose √ will assist you to reduce stress and stop gambling.

____

____

____

____

____

____

____

____

____

____

____

____

____

____

GAMBLING AND AWARENESS

We motivate ourselves by improving insight into our self-defeated, self-destructive attitudes and behaviors, and by genuinely retaining awareness of what we really want from life.

Are you determined to change your life for the better? Do you want to remain focus on the positive aspects of life? Can you motivate, educate, and empower yourself? Are you ready to change and apply self-control? Are you confident about your abilities to remain free of gambling?   YES/NO

1. Think about your **LAST** problem due to gambling? What happened?

____

____

____

____

2. What could you have **DONE** differently?

____

____

____

____

3. How the problem started?

____

____

____

____

4. **How many times did you promise yourself not to lose self-control? Please elaborate about situations that you lost self-control and started gambling.**

0	1	2	3	4	5	6	7	8	9	10	+

____

____

____

____

5. What is going to be different **NOW**?

____

____

____

____

6. Have you been impatient? YES/NO. Please explain.

____

____

____

____

7. Identify seven **SITUATIONS** you must avoid in order to remain free of gambling.

1. ____

2. ____

3. ____

4. ____

5. ____

6. ____

7. ____

8. Identify five **PEOPLE** you must avoid in order to remain free of gambling.

1.____

2.____

3.____

4.____

5.____

9. Identify three **PLACES** you must avoid in order to remain free of gambling

1.____

2.____

3.____

10. Identify three **DECISIONS** you must **MAKE DAILY** in order to remain free of gambling.

1.____

2.____

3.____

11. Identify three **HIGH RISK BEHAVIORS** you must avoid in order to remain free of gambling.

1.____

2.____

3.____

12. Identify the name of three **PEOPLE** you can reach for support when you feel the urge to gamble.

1.____

2.____

3.____

13. Identify four **HEALTHY** coping skills that you must use when you feel the urge to gamble.

1.____

2.____

3.____

4.____

14. Identify four **UNHEALTHY** ways you must **AVOID** when you feel the desire to gamble.

1.____

2.____

3.____

4.____

15. Identify the name of three **PLACES** you may go when you feel the desire to gamble.

1.____

2.____

3.____

16. Identify three **PHYSICAL** signs of **STRESS** that may trigger you to gamble. Please explain.

1.____

2.____

3.____

17. Identify three **EMOTIONAL** signs of **STRESS** that may trigger you to gamble. Please explain. (e.g. sadness, fear, pain, excessive worrying))

1.____

2.____

3.____

18. Identify three **MENTAL** signs of **STRESS** that may trigger you to gamble. Please explain. (e.g. lack of assertiveness, lack of confidence)

1.____

2.____

3.____

GAMBLING AND LIFESTYLE

A lifestyle is a way of living and a way of life with certain habits, attitudes, morals, principles, economic status, and other aspects that may shape an individual or a group. Sometimes people need to change everything in order to remain free of trouble. The changes may include employment, friendships, location, environment, diet, belief system, partnerships, relationships, and other aspects that have directly or indirectly impact on their lives.

1. Does your lifestyle attract trouble? YES/NO. Please elaborate.

____

____

2. How motivated are you to change your LIFESTYLE? Please circle one.

0	1	2	3	4	5	6	7	8	9	10

Not Motivated   **100% Motivated**

3. What do you **NEED** to change about your lifestyle?

____

____

4. What do you **WANT** to change about your lifestyle?

____

____

5. What **WOULD** you change about your lifestyle?

____

____

6. What **CAN** you change about your lifestyle?

____

____

7. What **MUST** you change about your lifestyle?

____

____

____

GAMBLING, STRESS AND WARNING SIGNS

We change our normal way of living due to the demands of stress, and may feel physically, emotionally, mentally, and spiritually overwhelmed.

1. **When you are stressed, your mind is** ________________________________

0	1	2	3	4	5	6	7	8	9	10

Clear Mind   **Trouble Thinking Clear**

Before your last gambling behavior   Please circle one

a) Did you think about the same over and over?	YES/NO
b) Did you dream about winning?	YES/NO
c) Did you have mood swings?	YES/NO
d) Did you have trouble controlling yourself?	YES/NO
e) Did you have trouble managing daily stress?	YES/NO
f) Did you feel shame or guilt?	YES/NO
g) Did you feel easily frustrated or irritated?	YES/NO
h) Did you feel hopeless, anxious, and depressed?	YES/NO
i) Did you think about traumatic experiences?	YES/NO
j) Did you think people would appreciate you more if you won?	YES/NO
k) Did you magically think of winning?	YES/NO
l) Did you feel bored?	YES/NO
m) Did you feel that you care only about gambling?	YES/NO
n) Did you feel sorrow about your life?	YES/NO
o) Did you feel that you were alone?	YES/NO
p) Did you feel that you didn't have any alternatives but gamble?	YES/NO
q) Did you feel you need a challenge?	YES/NO
r) Did you neglect self-control?	YES/NO
t) Did you feel social pressure?	YES/NO
u) Did you have any changes on your sleeping patterns?	YES/NO
v) Did you feel that you needed to have more fun?	YES/NO
w) Were you in the company of friends?	YES/NO

Please complete

- *Before my I last gamble* ________________________________

____

____

2. How many questions have you answered: YES____________ NO___________
   Reflect and explain your answers.

____

____

____

____

____

____

____

____

____

____

3. How do you react to stress?

Physically: (e.g. Lack of energy, sleep disturbances)

____

____

____

____

Emotionally/Mentally: (e.g. irritability, nervousness, edginess)

____

____

____

____

____

Behaviorally: (e.g. angry outbursts, less sleep)

____

____

____

____

____

____

4. Identify your daily, weekly, monthly, yearly stressors.

Daily:

____

____

____

Explain: ____

____

____

____

Weekly:

____

____

____

Explain: ____

____

____

____

Monthly:

____

____

____

____

Explain: ____

____

____

____

Yearly:

____

____

____

____

Explain: ____

____

____

5. How can you **MANAGE** stress? Please identify at least seven ways you can manage and reduce stress. (e.g. plan your time, prioritize, organize, exercise, speak with a friend, apply relaxation and meditation techniques)

1.____

2.____

3.____

4.____

5.____

6.____

7.____

ADDICTION, CONFLICTS AND RESOLUTION

Addiction, including gambling creates self-conflict and conflict with others. Fears, manipulation, and deception may generate conflicts. We must understand the roots of conflicts that may arise from differences. We must be aware of our needs, and figure out why we are truly in conflict with ourselves and others. Conflict must encourage us to examine issues wisely and inspire solutions. The turmoil of our values, perceptions, desires, ideas, morals, beliefs, attitudes, and tendencies are fuel for our conflicts. When in conflict with others, we must be mindful of our emotions and behaviors, and try to comprehend the emotions and behaviors of others, in a calm, relaxed, consistent, fair and alert way. We must pay attention to nonverbal communication and entertain win/win resolutions.

1. Have you been troubled due to conflicts with a person? (e.g. your partner) YES/NO. Please explain.

____

____

____

____

____

2. Have you been in conflict with your inner self? (e.g. daily contradictions, struggle with decisions) YES/NO. Please explain.

____

____

____

____

____

3. Do you feel uncomfortable, stressed, or agitated when you are in conflict with yourself or others? YES/NO. Please explain.

____

____

____

____

____

4. Are you able to think about positive outcomes when in conflict with others? YES/NO. Please explain.

____

____

____

____

____

____

5. How do you resolve a conflict with somebody? Do you effectively listen? Do you reflect about what is being said or done to resolve the conflict? Please explain how you have resolved a personal conflict?

____

____

____

____

____

____

____

____

____

____

6. When in conflict with others, do you clarify, acknowledge, discuss, and establish common goals that are beneficial to both parties? YES/NO. Please illustrate by explaining a conflict you have had in the past.

____

____

____

____

____

____

7. Are you able to identify barriers to resolve a conflict, and in a positive, calm way, agree about how to resolve the conflict? YES/NO. Please illustrate by explaining a conflict you have had.

____

____

____

____

____

____

8. Would you take responsibility and accountability for a conflict? YES/NO. Please illustrate by explaining a conflict that had a resolution.

____

____

____

____

____

____

9. How capable are you in finding a RESOLUTION for a conflict?

Please circle one

0	**1**	**2**	**3**	**4**	**5**	**6**	**7**	**8**	**9**	**10**
Not capable										**Extremely capable**

Please explain your answer:

____

____

____

____

RELATIONSHIPS

Addiction, including gambling affects relationships. Relationships are necessary in our society. Healthy relationships have a great impact in the prevention of conflict. We may or may not have a healthy relationship with ourselves, our family, our co-workers, or with our partner due to gambling or other factors. Our perceptions about our healthy or unhealthy relationships may vary with our belief system and the level of acceptance or denial. Unhealthy relationships sometimes deliver enough force of shame, guilt, frustration, pain, resentment, and annoyance to give up harmony and hope. A healthy connection between people must be based on mutual respect, trust, loyalty, good communication, honesty, and a sense of own identity and care.

1. In your opinion, what makes a healthy relationship? (e.g. mutual respect)

____

____

____

2. In your opinion, what makes an unhealthy relationship? (e.g. attempt to control or manipulate others)

____

____

____

3. What makes a healthy romantic relationship? Please choose √ what you agree.

Write other

☐ **Fairness**	☐ **Support**	☐ **Ability to express**	☐ ______
☐ **Love**	☐ **Consistency**	☐ **No violence**	☐ ______
☐ **Arguments**	☐ **Good communication**	☐ **Feeling of safety**	☐ ______
☐ **Mental stress**	☐ **Sincerity**	☐ **No fear**	☐ ______
☐ **Instigation**	☐ **Honesty**	☐ **Appreciation**	☐ ______
☐ **Nagging**	☐ **Mutual respect**	☐ **Care**	☐ ______
☐ **Gossip**	☐ **Humor**	☐ **Connection**	☐ ______
☐ **Over reaction**	☐ **Sense of identity**	☐ **Happiness**	☐ ______
☐ **Silence**	☐ **Validation**	☐ **Use of drugs**	☐ ______

Please discuss your choices with your therapist or in group.

Please choose if you agree or disagree with statements

When I am in a romantic relationship

1.	I care only about myself	AGREE	DISAGREE
2.	I feel secure and appreciated	AGREE	DISAGREE
3.	I don't laugh much or feel happy	AGRRE	DISAGREE
4.	I have weekly arguments	AGREE	DISAGREE
5.	I gamble with my partner	AGREE	DISAGREE
6.	I usually attempt to control and manipulate	AGREE	DISAGREE
7.	I feel pressure to please my partner all the time	AGREE	DISAGREE
8.	I have a lack of privacy	AGREE	DISAGREE
9.	I feel controlled and victimized	AGREE	DISAGREE
10.	I am unable to work or be independent	AGREE	DISAGREE
11.	I have limited access to my family	AGREE	DISAGREE
12.	I don't have too many friendships	AGREE	DISAGREE
13.	I worry about my future	AGREE	DISAGREE
14.	I don't make too many decisions	AGREE	DISAGREE
15.	I lack confidence about my future	AGREE	DISAGREE
16.	I am happy	AGREE	DISAGREE
17.	I respect my partner	AGREE	DISAGREE
18.	I trust my partner	AGREE	DISAGREE
19.	I am loyal to my partner	AGREE	DISAGREE
20.	I have affairs	AGREE	DISAGREE
21.	I don't trust my partner	AGREE	DISAGREE
22.	I hide my gambling from my partner	AGREE	DISAGREE
23.	I feel lonely	AGREE	DISAGREE
24.	I am overwhelmed	AGREE	DISAGREE
25.	I break the law	AGREE	DISAGREE

Please discuss your answers with your therapist or in group.

THE IMPORTANCE OF A BALANCED LIFE

**Addiction, including gambling, affects the balance and harmony of your life.
A balanced life is a life well lived. We seek balance in so many aspects of our lives
because we want to feel free of stress, and enjoy the elements of this world with a
clear mind set. We must look at our life and fully understand its blue print, purpose
and direction. We must assess our goals, plans, and objectives and reflect about how
to accomplish them by balancing external (e.g. work, family, friendships,
responsibilities) and internal (e.g. health, mind, gratification, self-reward) forces.
Our true happiness is always shaped by balance.**

We must empower and motivate ourselves in order to have a healthy life.

1. Is your life balanced? YES/NO. Please explain.

____

____

____

____

____

2. How balanced do you feel with your family time? Do you spend enough time with
    your family? YES/NO. Please explain.

____

____

____

____

____

3. Do you spend enough time by yourself? YES/NO. Please explain.

____

____

____

____

____

4. How do you motivate yourself to live free of addiction?

____

____

____

____

____

____

5. What should you do to balance your life?

____

____

____

____

____

6. What activities must you decrease or increase in order to find balance in your life? Please explain.

____

____

____

____

____

7. What can you do in one week to initiate the process of balancing your life?

____

____

____

____

____

8. Are you able to connect with your inner self and enjoy life free of addiction?
    YES/NO. Please explain.

____

____

____

____

____

9. Who can help you to balance your life?

____

____

____

10. Name at least 5 healthy ways to increase balance in your life.

    1.____

    2.____

    3.____

    4.____

    5.____

- **How BALANCED is your life today?**

Please circle one

0	**1**	**2**	**3**	**4**	**5**	**6**	**7**	**8**	**9**	**10**
Not balanced					**Half balanced**					**Extremely balanced**

Please explain your choice.

____

____

____

____

____

MINDFULNESS IS NOW

Mindfulness is the state of being conscious, completely awake, and fully attentive to the internal and external elements of the present moment. When we are awake from our daily automatic life, we start living what appears to be a surreal dimension of reality. We understand and appreciate the interconnection of everything without judging or falling for life distractions (e.g. politics, sports, organized religion). We have insight and we are insight of the present moment. When we achieve a sublime mindfulness approach to life, we experience great freedom and quality of living. We are no longer conditioned to act and react on auto-pilot. We make wiser choices because we are _awake_. The practice of mindfulness assists us to identify and increase self- control and awareness of impulsive, automatically destructive, addictive, risky behaviors.

1. Do you have awareness of your thoughts, attitudes and behaviors that may lead to gamble? YES/NO. Please explain.

____

____

____

____

____

____

2. Have you decided in an automatic and impulsive way to gamble? YES/NO. Please elaborate about past situations.

____

____

____

____

____

3. Are you able to pause, recognize, and challenge emotional experiences that may lead to gambling? YES/NO. Please explain.

____

____

____

____

____

4. Are you able to pause, acknowledge, understand, and be nonjudgmental towards yourself and your experiences? YES/NO. Please explain.

____

____

____

____

____

5. Are you always conscious of your emotions, actions, reactions and behaviors? YES/NO. Please explain.

____

____

____

____

____

____

6. What can you do to remain attentive to your desires and impulsive behaviors?

____

____

____

____

7. How much mindful / aware are you right NOW?

Please circle one

0	**1**	**2**	**3**	**4**	**5**	**6**	**7**	**8**	**9**	**10**
Not at all										**Extremely**

Please explain your answer:

____

____

____

____

____

<h1 style="text-align:center">ALWAYS MINDFULNESS</h1>

Please circle

1. Do you find it hard to pay attention to the things you say or do?	YES	NO
2. Have you got in trouble because of your impulsive decisions?	YES	NO
3. Do you have difficulty paying attention during tasks?	YES	NO
4. Do you multi-task?	YES	NO
5. Do you act before you think of the consequences?	YES	NO
6. Are you worried about the future or the past?	YES	NO
7. Do you tend to forget daily responsibilities?	YES	NO
8. Do you have difficulty enjoying the present moment?	YES	NO
9. Do you have fun with friends?	YES	NO
10. Are you able to relax?	YES	NO
11. Are you easily distracted by the media?	YES	NO
12. Do you sometimes forget about your responsibilities?	YES	NO
13. Are you easily influence by others?	YES	NO
14. Have you got in trouble in due to peer pressure?	YES	NO
15. Do you try to enjoy every moment of the day?	YES	NO
16. Are you attentive to what is happening NOW?	YES	NO

Please reflect, elaborate, and discuss your answers.

____

____

____

____

____

____

____

____

____

MAKING DECISIONS

Any decision we make is ultimately our decision. Every day we make wise, average, or poor decisions. Every morning we decide to move on with our daily routine or do something different. Sometimes we decide things without much thinking, and sometimes we pause and think about what will be the best decision. We may move automatically like every other day, or we may reflect about the decision to make. Decision making may be facilitated by emotional, physical, or spiritual experiences, by measuring options and consequences, by perception of pros and cons, by acquiring brainstorming knowledge, by revising and reviewing, by describing and planning, and by values, needs, attitudes, and behaviors.

1. You decided to stop gambling. What makes this decision **NECESSARY** for you? Please explain your answer.

____

____

____

____

____

2. You decided to pursue your personal goals, desires and dreams with a clear-headed mind, and focus on your self-control. What are the **BENEFITS** of this decision? Please explain your answer.

____

____

____

____

____

3. What were the most difficult decisions you have made when you lacked self-control? What were the **CONSEQUENCES** of gambling? Please explain your answer.

____

____

____

____

____

4. What was the most irrational decision you made when gambling? What were the
    CONSEQUENCES? Please explain your answer.

____

____

____

____

____

____

5. Please write seven decisions you made when you were gambling, and how those
    decisions **AFFECTED** your life.

1. ____

2. ____

3. ____

4. ____

5. ____

6. ____

7. ____

6. Would you make the same decisions NOW? Please elaborate.

____

____

____

____

____

____

____

____

7. Please write seven **UNHEALTHY** choices you made when you were gambling, which resulted in consequences that you did **NOT EXPECT**. Please explain.

1.____

2.____

3.____

4.____

5.____

6.____

7.____

8. Would you make the same choices **NOW?** Please explain.

____

____

____

____

____

9. How many times have your **IMPULSIVE** decisions resulted in chaos? Please explain.

____

____

____

____

____

10. How many times have your **THOUGHTFUL** decisions resulted in chaos? Please explain.

____

____

____

____

____

11. What are the **PROS and CONS** of making a decision after carefully calculating the consequences? Please explain.

____

____

____

____

____

12. **How do you make a choice or a decision?** Write an example of a decision you made today, and explain in detail why and how you came to the decision. Please write the consequences of your decision, pros and cons, and possible alternatives.

____

____

____

____

____

____

____

13. **How capable are you of making WISE and beneficial decisions?**

Please circle one

0	1	2	3	4	5	6	7	8	9	10

Not capable   **Extremely capable**

Please explain your answer.

____

____

____

____

____

____

____

SOLVING PROBLEMS

We will encounter problems during our lives. Sometimes we will have minor problems, and sometimes unthinkable problems. Problems exist, and we are able to resolve them by first identifying symptoms of the problem, seeking information about the problem, brainstorming answers for the problem, choosing the most beneficial resolution for the problem, visualizing and clarifying a plan to resolve the problem, reviewing the proposal to resolve the problem, and putting in action the most positive solution for the problem.

1. When does a **SYMPTOM** of a problem become a problem? (*e.g. thinking about gambling)*

____

____

____

____

2. Are you able to understand symptoms of your personal issues before they become **UNMANAGEABLE** problems? Please write about a problem you had and how you dealt with it.

____

____

____

____

3. Usually, do you **RESOLVE** your problems by yourself, or do you ask for help? Please explain by using an example of a problem you are currently facing.

____

____

____

____

4. Do you **MINIMIZE** your problems? Do you make your problems smaller than they are? YES/NO. Please explain.

____

____

____

____

5. Please list five **PROBLEMS** caused by your gambling.

    1.____

    2.____

    3.____

    4.____

    5.____

6. Please list five ways in which you attempted to **CONVINCE** others that you did not have a problem with gambling.

    1.____

    2.____

    3.____

    4.____

    5.____

7. Are you **NOW** aware of the impact of the problems caused by your gambling and how it affected you and the people who care about you? YES/NO. In detail, clarify the impact of the problems caused by your gambling.

____

____

____

____

____

8. How capable are you in resolving your problems?

Please circle one

0	**1**	**2**	**3**	**4**	**5**	**6**	**7**	**8**	**9**	**10**	**+**

Not capable   **Extremely capable**

Please explain your answer: ______________________________________

____

SPIRITUAL JOURNEY

How we view our own existence in the universe is what makes us aware of our actions and reactions to everything. Our physical existence constantly reinvents its time and connects our bodies and souls to the universe. We are the energy that the universe uses to magically and patiently evolve through us. Our bodies are a process that never stands still, and our souls are vessels seeking enlightenment by connecting and feeling the world physically, socially, emotionally, and spiritually.

Our souls constantly animate our bodies and seek balance, harmony, meaning, serenity, purpose, self-actualization, and satisfaction. We are the mindfulness conscience that brings change by letting go of our old limited beliefs. We meditate and seek positive change in our inner selves by embracing our body and soul towards the awakening of compassion, empathy, goodness, and love. We are souls that use bodies. We belong to the multi-level dimensions of the universe.

1. **How do you view your own spiritual existence in the universe? Please circle one.**

0	1	2	3	4	5	6	7	8	9	10
Do not										Extremely

Some Spiritual Principles:

Honesty	**Gratitude**	**Tolerance**	**Love**
Acceptance	**Forgiveness**	**Give more**	**Care**
Surrender	**Patience**	**Except less**	**Compassion**
Accept Change	**Live simple**	**Live humbly**	**Self-actualization**

2. What do you think gives meaning to your life?

____

____

____

____

3. Do you consider yourself spiritual? YES/NO. Please explain.

____

____

____

____

4. If YES, how important is your spiritual belief? Please explain.

____

____

5. Have you ever had a spiritual awakening? YES/NO. Please describe.

____

____

____

6. Do you talk about spirituality or religion with someone? YES/NO. If, yes, who
    and when?

____

____

____

7. Do you believe that spiritual and religious practices enhance the functioning of
    the brain in ways that improve physical and emotional health? YES/NO. Please
    explain.

____

____

____

8. Do you think that contemplation about God and other spiritual values awakens
    our conscience and enhances the sensory perceptions about the Self?
    YES/NO. Please explain.

____

____

____

9. Think about your body and how it works. Write about a physical illness that you
    have experienced and the events that followed.

____

____

____

____

____

10. Do you attend self-help groups? YES/NO. Please explain.

____

____

____

11. Are you conscious or aware of the impact of gambling in your body, mind, and soul? YES/NO. Please explain.

____

____

____

12. Are you able to practice mindfulness meditation by putting aside thoughts of the past and future, and staying in the present moment? YES/NO. Please explain.

____

____

____

13. Are you interested in learning more about meditation and relaxation techniques? YES/NO. If you answered yes, explain how beneficial it will be for you to know more about meditation and relaxation techniques.

____

____

____

____

Discuss with your psychotherapist, ways to obtain information and learn more about meditation and relaxation techniques. You will enjoy a unique self-reflection experience, by cleansing your mind from accumulated thoughts.

The mind, soul and body are uniquely designed to be in harmony with each other, and through meditation, we are able to travel into a mindfulness conscience in a clear, wiser, focused, and profound way.

WORDS AND ACTIONS

Do not be afraid of life. Always believe in yourself.

I thought about this statement when shaping many of my thoughts, and attitudes. My inner voice built confidence and assured me that life is worth living. We must appreciate a life of value, confidence, determination, courage, virtue, and understand that fear only exists to be conquered. Fear may become the greatest fertilizer to intensify our personal success.

We can, and we will conquer our fears by BELIEVING and KNOWING ourselves.

WHAT YOU ARE AND WHAT YOU ARE SUPPOSED TO BE

We are what we think, and our thoughts can be believable to us and others. We have a blue print to follow and determine where our life must go. We exist to live our lives not as an idea of living, but as a reality to accomplish. Our dreams, plans, and goals have more reasons for us to pursue them, than to let them fade away. We must embrace basic principles and deeply believe in ourselves.

CHANGE

Change is not always wanted, accepted, or respected. We must connect with our emotions in order to understand our actions, and modify our behaviors. We must not ignore our needs to avoid changing our destructive behaviors. We must not forget the execution of forgiveness to avoid change.

Change is what connects the universe, and we are part of it. Accept, embrace, and understand that change is a beneficial element of life.

GRIEF AND LOSS

Life sometimes brings us unthinkable pain due to grief and loss. We may lose a loved one, a close relationship, a pet, a friend, a job, a lover, our own health, or something or someone we care a lot. We may feel angry, depressed, anxious, and dreamlike. We may avoid feelings of sadness and despair by taking the path of denial, which may result in substance abuse, mental illness, and health problems. We neglect ourselves and others, and question our ways mentally and spiritually. We may feel lost in the realm wheel of magic, test the boundaries of sanity, and our capacity to remain human.

Loss may change our ways of thinking, and generate emotions and physical reactions that we have never experienced.

Grief is a natural reaction to loss. Grief can take away our sense of belonging to something or someone, and we may feel sad, scared, and lonely. People grieve differently, depending on their life experiences, personality traits, faith, learned coping skills, support system, type of loss, or other factors.

Any loss can cause grief including:

- Death of a loved one
- Loss of a relationship
- Loss of own physical or mental health
- Loss of work or job
- Loss of financial stability
- Loss of possessions or property
- Loss of a loved place or stable home
- Loss of a child moving away

- An injury or disability
- Loss of a friend
- Loss of a lifestyle
- Miscarriage
- Loss of a plan or dream
- Loss of safety
- Loss of faith
- Other_____________________

By grieving we naturally accept loss, and heal by expressing our feelings and utilizing our support system. Do not be afraid to ask for help. Do not limit your tears. You must feel to heal.

We must start the healing process by acknowledging the roots of pain, and conquer the abysm of suffering.

The death of a loved one might encourage you to assess your own feelings about mortality. Grief and loss are personal and we must understand our emotions, seek our support system, and feel the natural process of healing without any resistance or delay.

1. Please reflect on who or what you have lost during your life.

____

____

____

____

____

____

2. Please list the emotions, thoughts and body changes you have had since your loss.

____

____

____

____

____

____

3. How has your loss affected your social life?

____

____

____

4. How has your loss affected your self-respect?

____

____

____

____

5. How has your loss affected your behaviors?

____

____

____

____

____

6. How has your loss affected your relationships?

____

____

____

____

____

7. Did you gamble, use drugs or alcohol because of the death of a love one?
    YES/NO. Please explain.

____

____

____

____

____

8. Did you have difficulty dealing with emotions and thoughts of loss?
    YES/NO. Please explain.

____

____

____

____

____

____

MY FUTURE BELONGS TO ME

Summarize your plans and goals to maintain self-control and meet your needs.

TO IMPROVE THE RELATIONSHIP WITH MYSELF

I will____

____

____

____

TO FIND OR MAINTAIN EMPLOYMENT

I will____

____

____

____

TO FIND OR MAINTAIN HOUSING

I will____

____

____

____

TO PURSUE EDUCATION OR VOCATIONAL SKILLS

I will____

____

____

____

TO HANDLE URGES AND CRAVINGS TO GAMBLE

I will____

____

____

____

TO HAVE OR MAINTAIN MEANS OF TRANSPORTATION

I will____

____

____

TO GAIN OR MAINTAIN A HEALTHY RELATIONSHIP WITH FAMILY

I will____

____

____

TO GAIN OR MAINTAIN A HEALTHY RELATIONSHIP WITH FRIENDS

I will____

____

____

TO LEARN MORE ABOUT MYSELF AND LIFE IN GENERAL

I will____

____

____

TO HAVE FUN AND ENJOY LIFE FREE OF CONFLICTS

I will____

____

____

____

TO REGULARLY UTILIZE MY SUPPORT SYSTEM

I will____

____

____

TO GAIN, MAINTAIN, AND EXPAND A HEALTHY SOCIAL NETWORK

I will____

____

____

____

____

TO REDUCE STRESS

I will____

____

____

____

____

TO ELIMINATE CHAOS IN MY LIFE

I will____

____

____

____

TO INCREASE RESPONSIBILITY FOR MY ACTIONS

I will____

____

____

____

TO APPLY PAUSE BEFORE REACTING

I will____

____

____

____

TO RECOGNIZE CONFLICTS

I will____

____

____

____

____

TO SAVE MONEY

I will____

____

____

____

____

____

Please add.

TO ____

I will____

____

____

____

TO ____

I will____

____

____

____

____

	Describe problem symptoms/behaviors/ attitudes/addictions/ obsessions/compulsions and other matters that you would like to change	How you will resolve/change/improve /eliminate? By doing what? Short Term Goals	Time Frame How long will it take to achieve the Short Term Goals?	How you will resolve/change/improve /eliminate? By doing what? Long Term Goals	Time Frame How long will take to achieve Long Term Goals?
1.					
2.					
3.					
4.					
5.					
6.					
7.					

1. Please elaborate about the benefits of your short and long-term goals, and current achievements.

____

____

____

____

____

____

____

____

____

____

____

2. Who can you ask to help you achieve your goals?

____

____

____

____

- **How CONFIDENT are you in achieving your short and long term goals? Please circle one.**

0	1	2	3	4	5	6	7	8	9	10
Not Confidence										Extremely Confidence

Please explain your answer.

____

____

____

____

____

SELF-CARE

We care about others and easily forget about ourselves. Self-care is care provided by you to yourself. You need to identify your beneficial needs and wants, and fulfill your desires and wishes. You need to assure yourself that you are healthy physically, mentally, emotionally, and spiritually.

You need to connect with nature, write a card to a love one, get a massage, meditate in your favorite place, exercise regularly, breath fresh and clean air, listen to music, enjoy a great book, watch a good movie, have fun, spoil yourself with things you can afford, energize yourself with a balanced diet, sleep well, take a nap and rest your body and mind, learn something new, and spend time with true friends who make you laugh.

1. Have you neglected your self-care? YES/NO. Please elaborate.

____

____

____

____

2. When was the last time you have done something for yourself? Please elaborate.

____

____

____

____

3. Have you cared for others and neglected yourself? YES/NO. Please elaborate.

____

____

____

____

4. How do you describe the behaviors that made you care less about yourself?

____

____

____

____

5. What can you do to increase self-care?

____

____

____

____

6. Please list the people, things, and places that you care about. Why?

____

____

____

____

7. Have you neglected yourself in order to care about others? YES/NO. Please
    explain.

____

____

____

8. When was the last time you visited your primary doctor? ________________
9. When was the last time you visited your dentist? ____________________
10. When was the last time you had a massage? ______________________
11. When was the last time you spoiled yourself? ____________________
12. When was the last time you laughed and had fun? __________________
13. When was the last time you felt good about yourself? ________________
14. When was the last time you loved being you? ____________________
15. When was the last time you smiled at a stranger? __________________
16. When was the last time you were able to relax and feel peace? ___________
17. When was the last time you felt positive about yourself? _______________

18. **How much do you love and care about yourself NOW? Please circle one.**

____

0   1   2   3   4   5   6   7   8   9   10   +

Do not   **Extremely Love & Care**
Love or Care

Please reflect about your answer.

____

____

____

HEALING WHEN JOURNALING

I encourage you to journal every day. Journaling has a charming effect.

Healing may use reflection and mindfulness observations by seeking words to describe our goals, strengths, weakness, thoughts, feelings, actions, and attitudes. We may write about our pains, ambitions and dreams, aggressively, patiently or sensitively on paper. Paper takes all types of ink, and any color. We may express our ability to perceive and process our inner selves by constructing awareness of life experiences. We may conclude ideas and re-build self-esteem, self-confidence, and self-determination by reactivating memories and recreating positive and less positive moments. We will teach ourselves by journaling. We may heal, learn, organize, transform, change, create, meditate, recall, imagine, improve, build, re-build, and restore our lives by journaling.

My Journal:

DAILY GAMBLING METER

Today is a good day.

Today is ________________________________ Date: ____________________

What was the highest number you reached on the gambling meter today?

- **How much did you gamble today?**

0	1	2	3	4	5	6	7	8	9	10	+

I did not gamble | | | | | | | | | | I gambled a lot today

1. **What triggered your highest number on the gambling meter?**

____

____

____

2. **What would you have done different?** ________________________

____

____

____

3. **Were you able to pause, and apply healthy decision making coping skills? YES/NO Please explain.**

____

4. **Did you apply self-control? YES/NO** ________________________

5. **Please write the signs that you were able to identify when you felt like gambling:**

Physical signs: ____

Mental signs: ____

Emotional signs: ____

Behavioral signs: ____

Comments: ____

____

____

Reflect and discuss your daily events and comments in group and with your psychotherapist. Make copies of this blank sheet and use it daily.

WEEKLY GAMBLING METER

Today is a good day.

Week from: ___________________ **To:** ___________________

What was the highest number you reached on the gambling meter this week?

0	1	2	3	4	5	6	7	8	9	10 +
I did not gamble										I gambled a lot

___	___	___	___	___	___	___
M	T	W	TH	F	S	S

What happened? Please elaborate.

Monday: ____

Tuesday: ____

Wednesday: ____

Thursday: ____

Friday: ____

Saturday: ____

Sunday: ____

1. **What was the event that triggered the highest number?**

____

____

2. **What would you have done different?** _______________________

____

3. **Please write the signs that you were able to identify when you gamble:**

Physical signs: ____

Mental signs: ____

Emotional signs: _______________________________________

Behavioral signs: ______________________________________

Reflect and discuss your weekly and daily events and comments in group and with your psychotherapist. Make copies of this blank sheet and use it weekly.

CONTRACT

I, ____ agree to learn coping
skills to deal with my addiction and demonstrate knowledge of self-control.

_______ (initials) I agree to care for myself, to eat well, and to get enough sleep each night.

_______ (initials) I agree to complete my daily and weekly gambling meter sheets.

_______ (initials) I agree to utilize my social support and community resources.

_______ (initials) I agree that, if I need help I will contact the following individuals:

____

____

____

_______ (initials) I agree to learn and demonstrate knowledge of application of problem

      solving, anger management , stress management, decision making, conflict

      resolution, and healthy communication coping skills.

_______ (initials) I agree to pause and wisely reflect before acting.

_______ (initials) I agree to the following conditions: _______________________

____

____

____

_______ (initials) I agree that these conditions are important, and worth following.

_______ (initials) I agree that this is a contract that I am willing to follow.

_______ (initials) I agree to honor this contract.

Signed____Date______________

Witnessed by_____________________________________Date______________

FEEDBACK

Please send me your suggestions, questions, observations, and comments. You may assist us in improving future publications. We are open to constructive criticism and appreciate your experience and insight.

Thank you.

Please contact me at rlima001@gmail.com

Please rate this workbook.

0	1	2	3	4	5	6	7	8	9	10
Terrible										Great

Please elaborate:

____

____

____

____

____

____

Suggestions:

____

____

____

____

____

____

____

____

____

____

NOTES

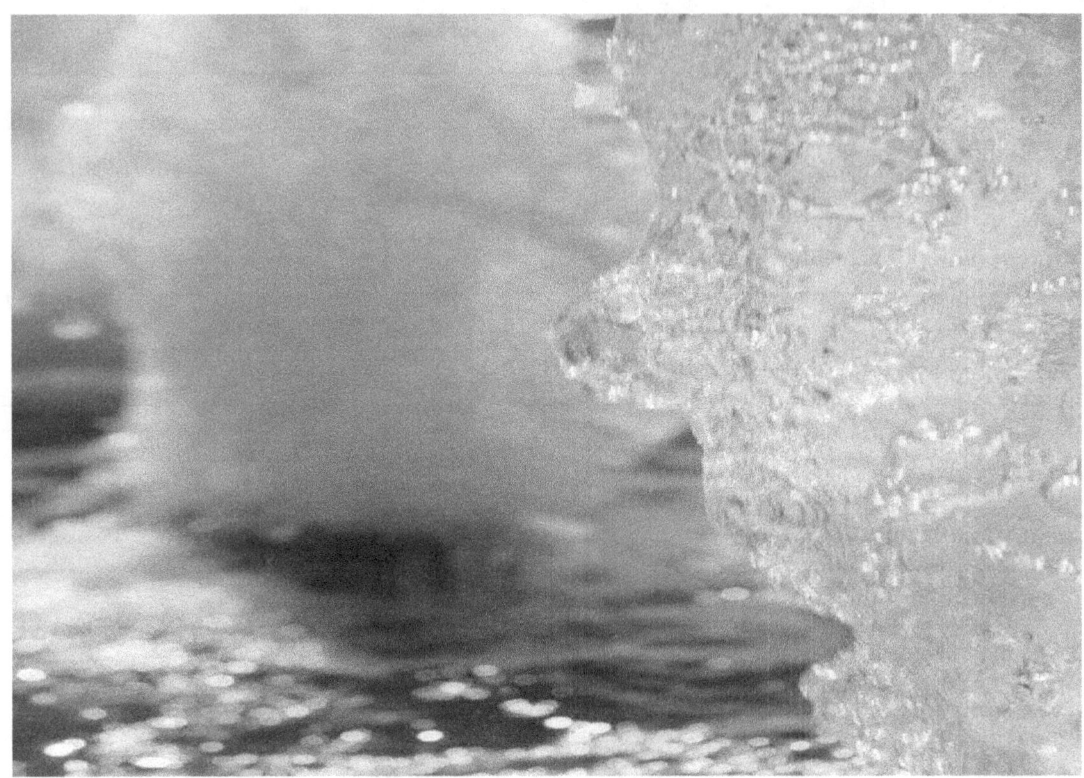

BE LIKE WATER

Water does not fight its way but finds a way. If you drop an open bottle of water on the floor, the water will not break the floor. The water will go around and into everything until it finds its destiny in a soft and calm way.

Adjusting to everything is a sublime experience. Accepting first that life is unfair is true awareness. Deciding to become part of your blue print or destiny is genuine understanding of your life purpose.

Increasing self-responsibility and self-accountability assist you to master and acquire self-determination. You are the shape of your thoughts and your actions are the result of such process.

No more blaming, no more excuses, no more denial, no more justifications, rationalizations, or minimizations. No more fakeness or lies. Apply what you know to be beneficial to you, and to what you love and care. Your purpose in life exists inside of you—now--.